The Phoenix Living Poets

KILROY WAS HERE

Poets Published in
The Phoenix Living Poets Series

★

JAMES AITCHISON

ALEXANDER BAIRD · ALAN BOLD

R. H. BOWDEN · FREDERICK BROADIE

GEORGE MACKAY BROWN · MICHAEL BURN

PHILIP CALLOW · HAYDEN CARRUTH

JOHN COTTON · JENNIFER COUROUCLI

GLORIA EVANS DAVIES

PATRIC DICKINSON

TOM EARLEY · D. J. ENRIGHT

IRENE FEKETE

JOHN FULLER · DAVID GILL

PETER GRUFFYDD

J. C. HALL · MOLLY HOLDEN

JOHN HORDER · P. J. KAVANAGH

RICHARD KELL · LAURIE LEE

LAURENCE LERNER

CHRISTOPHER LEVENSON

EDWARD LOWBURY · NORMAN MACCAIG

ROY MCFADDEN

DIANA MCLOGHLEN

JAMES MERRILL · RUTH MILLER

LESLIE NORRIS · ROBERT PACK

RODNEY PYBUS · ARNOLD RATTENBURY

ADRIENNE RICH · ANNE SEXTON · JON SILKIN

JON STALLWORTHY

EDWARD STOREY · TERENCE TILLER

SYDNEY TREMAYNE

JON MANCHIP WHITE

KILROY WAS HERE

Poems 1970-74

By

JOHN COTTON

CHATTO AND WINDUS

THE HOGARTH PRESS

1975

Published by
Chatto and Windus Ltd
with The Hogarth Press Ltd
42 William IV Street
London WC2

★

Clarke, Irwin & Co. Ltd.
Toronto

ISBN 0 7011 2089 4

© John Cotton 1975

Printed in Great Britain by
Lewis Reprints Ltd.
The Brown Knight and Truscott Group
London and Tonbridge

For TOBY and BEVIS,
together with the future

Acknowledgements are due to the editors of the following periodicals and publications in which certain of these poems have appeared:

Encounter; *Kaleidoscope*; *Limestone*; *New Statesman*; *Outposts*; *Poetry Review*; *Priapus*; *Second Aeon*; *Solstice*; *Tagus*; Phoenix Theatre Broadsheets, Leicester; The Opening Festival Booklet of the Ward Freeman School, Buntingford; The Sceptre Press Broadsheets; The Stroud Festival Guinness Poetry Competition.

Best S F 1972 (E.P. Putnam's, New York); The P.E.N. Anthology: *New Poems 1973—74* (Hutchinson); *Looking Glass: an anthology of contemporary poetry* (Edward Arnold).

Three of the 'photograph poems' (pages 21—23) appeared as a broadsheet published by John Fuller's Sycamore Press, Oxford, and 'Fragments' was published in *Poetry Chicago*.

CONTENTS

COLUMBUS ON ST. DOMINICA

('Columbus landed here for a day', Travelogue)

The men inland exploring
the island and its women,
it is a time to savour
the moment and its quality,
the air as soft as Spring
in Andalucia,
redolent with vegetation
and the moist richness of the sea.

Yet the expected sense
of triumph eludes me,
the elation of giving,
at last, two fingers
to the doubts of Saint Augustine,
resolved to a regret
astringent as the sharp
metallic taste of the water
running clear over these beds of pebbles.

For the moment of discovery
is irredeemable:
The first sighting of mountains,
the green profusion of valleys,
the echo of bird call
etching the morning,
to continue only
in the distorting mirror of the memory.

Such was the pristine
golden land we dreamt of,
our sin in landfall
to let slip once more
the chains of Knowledge.
And if I should return
it will be to the cliffs beyond,
gnawed by the sea,
where things crumble
and the only philosophy is erosion.

KILROY WAS HERE

"English had as his second-in-command of artillery another American, a man named Bradish, whose name can be seen now cut into the altar in the inner sanctuary at Abu Simbel. Little else is known of him."

The Blue Nile: Alan Moorehead.

Remember me:
the burden of Dido's lament;
and of those names we see
written or carved
in sometimes improbable places?
Well, the names are there
if not the faces.
Certainly it would seem true
of Bradish's
self-cut memorial.
Against the fear
of nothingness
I was here
plead all the Kilroys of this world:
Alexander's soldier
who left his Greek in Northern India,
and Desaix's men
who inscribed Dendera.
Then those suitably ephemeral
declarations of affection,
hearts and names
scratched on cactus leaves
on a cliff path in Spain:
Hans unt Beyb;
Teresa y Fernando;
and, touching in its mild chauvinism,
May and Bert, England.

11

DOGS

Bluey — that rightly famed Australian dog,
Waited his life out at the hospital
Where his swagman master had died.
Not knowing, Bluey hopefully eyed
All leavers for the return of a memory,
And we are filled with admiration
For such canine fidelity.
Yet there was another dog, Freud's chow
That cringed in a corner from the stench
Of his master's cancer. Can we allow
That dogs, too, prefer ideas to reality?

EN ROUTE

Every Sunday about ten
The cattle-truck with its living load,
On its way from Eynsham to the abattoir,
Parks at the cafe across the road
For the driver's tea break, when,
Between slats, liquid eyes fill
With the only light
In a darkness still
Redolent of fields and bright
Pastures. The morning air broken
By an alien lowing,
A lament, not so much
For where they are going
As for what they have left behind.

NEW TOWN BLUES

I. Culture

Near half a week's pay on the blonde bouffant
and a pair of thigh length boots,
she queens the fore-court
to lighten many a darkness.
A workman, pasting posters
for the town's Arts Festival,
draws breath at the callipygian exposé
as she bends to remove a petrol cap.
He is not one for minority pursuits.
She thinks of what to get the kids for tea.

II. Environment

Grandma constantly tells how, as a girl,
she held the horses in the fields,
wiped them down at the end of the day
and slept by them in the stable.
While her grandson,
cut off by regiments of streets
and a technology that ostracises him,
each Saturday on the way back from the pub
kicks in the bus-shelter to show them.
And they, as regularly, repair it in reply.

III. Social Services

At the shopping centre they sit on benches,
a refuge from a hostile domesticity.
Grey stubble above grubby neckbands,
redolent of pipes and weak bladders,
they fumble for matches with thickly veined hands
while they soak in the last of the summer.
Memories revived by the young wives
with their sturdy hams, they recall places
the authorities considered unsuitable.

IV. Romance

Through the day's chores
romance lies chrysalid
in plastic rollers
under the patterned headscarves.
Evening with its disco and lights
flirts with a world that cannot be theirs.
Realists, after a few Snowballs,
at the back of the parking lot
the hands in their pants
come by the courtesy of Red Barrel.

THE WILDERNESS

This is the wilderness my uncle said:
A corner of the garden he'd let go,
Grass waist high and trees grown spindly
Because they were too close together,
A contrast to the rose beds, well mown lawn
And ranks of vegetables. There we would play
Where Indians, outlaws and rugged pioneers
Haunted that patch of wonder surviving
In a suburb. It's all gone now: childhood, uncle,
The patch sold to more determined gardeners.
To remember is to miss that place
Where imagination grew, lost now
In the cautious cultivation of our days.
'All gardens should have one', uncle said,
We should have listened to him.

FIRE

A doubtful elm
and half a ton of wood
lopped limb by limb
filled the end of the garden.
After the initial blaze
the fire stood
smouldering, a glowing craze
through the white of ash
stirred by threats of flame
slicking the larger logs.

Just short of a week
we carried
its gift of smoke
in our clothing and nostrils:
and each night
it brooded in the dark,
interrupting its silences
in an upward crackle of spark
and flame as it shifted.

One night of broken sleep
I looked out at it.
There, in the deep
polarized light
of a haloed moon,
it breathed in the gloom
like some presiding spirit,
a sentinel reminding
of ancient watch
or bale fires that burn
as guardians from beasts and fantasies,
a reassurance to which
I made a prodigal return.

PRELUDES: SAN MARTIN

I
First light, the dogs
That signalled from farm to farm
Have fallen silent.

II
Stillness soaks the ancient stones,
The air settling
In the pervasion of mimosa.

III
In the ruined city the long dead
Lie too deep for the sun
That will drag its shadows over them;

IV
While the sea renews itself
Round the harbour they first built,
Salt air bringing an awareness of lungs.

V
Hallowing the morning, purple heron
Celebrate a eucharist of frogs
Before the disturbance of farmers.

VI
Warmth begins to fill the hollows,
And through the shirt's fabric
The flesh eases to the sun's beneficence.

VII
The sky, a blue that rings in the mind,
Is as clear as the new page
In the poet's notebook.

VIII
The day's preludes
When order seems a possibility.

PHOTOGRAPHY

How readily photographs capture
a certain kind of perfection: happy
family parties, the group on the beach,
or those advertisements in the colour
supplements where she sits at the mirror
to prepare for the evening, unblemished
and serene in the pristine uplift
of her underwear, bare toes buried
in a quicksand of carpet — just the right
touch of sex and opulence for selling
a kitchen stove — and never a hint
of the pain in her side or the worm already in the rose. Then there's that picture
of me on holiday, drinking Beaujolais
by the side of a lake which reflects
the ultimate grey of mountains. He's not
thinking of how he's going to pay for it
nor, for that matter, what in the end. I
look at the photograph and envy him.

KEITH DOUGLAS

'Simplify me when I'm Dead': Collected Poems

I lean against my car
and recall him in the photograph
leaning against military vehicle
Z4977485
in readiness for the desert.
Sleeves rolled and cap slightly askew,
he smiles as he poses,
the young hero in the wings of Europe,
alive in the frisson of fresh landfalls.
There's a simplicity for you,
which the poems will always deny.
To work without hope is not
to work hopelessly, he said:
A reassuring message from the dead.

GERTRUDE STEIN AND ALICE TOKLAS PLUS ONE

In the picture they are sitting in St. Mark's Square,
A pair of firm faced ladies of mature years,
Their voluminous dresses proclaiming the period.
The photograph fixes them, Gertrude and Alice,
Still remembered for their writings,
They have the look as if they sensed
They were being taken for posterity.
But what of the boy, in the sailor-suit,
Between them and the Cathedral in the background?
He, too, looks knowingly photographed.
Did he wonder about the two strangers
With whom he shared that moment?
Hardly expecting to appear,
Over a half a century later,
On the dust jacket of a book in England,
Could he even have considered the chance
Of such a vicarious immortality?
Long gone now, does someone remember him?

FIRST LOVE

A photograph moves one to remember
a face that was fading with time. Soft haired,
your slight figure fetching in a chequered frock,
you bask in the warmth of your sixteen years
in a garden forsaken now where weeds
run wild as memories. Are they still there,
the table and deck-chairs at the lawn's edge,
ready for tea where your eyes excited
the first and secret fermentations of love?
A never to be forgotten prelude
now in perspective, insubstantial
as the rotting canvas we once sat on.
But the spores of memory still latent,
stirred by the opening of an album,
the heart's affection moves towards you across time.

REUNION

'Can you recognize anyone here?' they said
Passing a group photograph:
And there she was still smouldering
Amongst a smiling anonymity.
Round her head
A halo of dark hair marking her out
As some malign benefactress,
Her blouse pulled tightly over all that malleability.
'Is it true that between her breasts?'
Then, with envy, 'How is it he knows?'
Because, because, once I was possessed,
And, I sense, somewhere the heady wine still flows
In secret arteries, waiting like those mines,
Rusting in the sand we once used as a bed,
For that innocent moment of my unwary tread.

OUTSIDE THE GATES OF EDEN

A leaden day, a strange town
And the lights against me,
It was by chance I was to see
Her leaning in a shop doorway. Her frown
Suggesting a boredom to come, she waited
To begin a Monday already mocking
Her week-end pretensions,
The seam of her temper awry as her stocking.

She looked up, and catching me looking, smiled.
I noticed her eyes, wistful, the curls
Of her hair piled,
The high cheeks of those Botticelli girls.
Even her dank mac could not disguise
The warm weight of her beauty.

For a moment we were one in surprise
Of that neat world where
Love is compassion and bodies
For pleasure, forgetful how rare
The escape from shoddy
Routine, duties or plain necessity.
Only the lights changed when I moved with the traffic.

OUT THERE

At any meeting
where the window
looks out on lawns or gardens
there is always a figure
trimming an edge
or seemingly working
at the sort of things
one might do in a shrubbery.
Behind a hedge
or at a distance
he may be hard to find:
but, like the requisite man
in a Chinese landscape painting,
you'll find him
if you look hard enough.
Is he, I wonder,
always the same man?
a spy or an emissary perhaps?
One day he will turn
to reveal his face.

FRAGMENTS

"This is the use of memory:
    For liberation."
T.S. Eliot: *Little Gidding*

As the plane rises, we watch the island
receding from us until we can hold it
complete in the eye; framed by water, its farms,
bays, hamlets and promontories scaled down
to a comprehensible map below us.
So in the cutting room of the mind
we work to distance experience
to meaningful proportions, to link
those fragments of memory that make us.

2.
Sundays are quiet. Across the railway
the row of terraced houses and the shop
on the corner, its air spiced by bread
and cough cure, a tin sign advertising
a tobacco not made for a generation.
The sharp click of heels on worn flags signals
a firmness of calf and thigh under bronzed nylon,
her morning errand bringing humanity
to brick and stone due for demolition.

3.
Some windows already boarded, as if
against a plague that will take all with it.
Even Provident Place is on the schedule.
One winter the canal froze and we walked it,
between locks, to the sound of church bells,
rejoicing in the temporary foot-way
and the luxury of gloves, until
called home by the smell of roast sweet on keen air.
Age is where places have immediate history:

4.
The canal; a pub recalling conversation
that proved a turning point; a bend in the lane

a poem that might have been written;
or a bus shelter flesh
warm under a fair-isle jersey, her breasts
like plump birds in the nest of her brassière.
Deep in us all the child whose habits
have survived fidelity and superstition,
and associations that will end with us.

5.
A day's drive across the Massif Central,
that evening we dine in warm southern air,
the lights of the small town sufficient
on the verandah. Time drifts with the music
from a radio across the way
where a girl waters a roof garden above
a shop. Time for reconciliation
while tired minds eased by good wine find order
as observers of a place not our own.

6.
From London fires spread a premature dawn
for suburbs where a thin rain of shrapnel
removes roof-tiles. For the young the advantage
of deserted streets and the blitz's black-out
to test the pulses of love. Recklessness or
a fine sense of values? As single-minded
the blood races towards the same warmth
to find a later reassurance
in the bonus of a winter's sunshine.

7.
Besieged by snow the house stands sentinel
against the night, the young child's breathing
a tenuous hold on life. Experience
began with the first open blouse; the fruit
that expelled from Eden? Redemption
long bought in domestic fires, the spread of flesh
that estuary towards which all runs
to be lost in the ultimate ocean.
The tide stirs with the child in the cot.

8.
In the bay ships nudge their way to harbour
the toll of bell-buoys a doubtful guide
in fog's peculiar claustrophobia
that gives even sound a new dimension,
and value to moments of clarity.
Then a face remembered. Though long past
and not known in any real sense of the word
the impression is there and its haunting tugs us.
We dare not look at our real wounds.

9.
The end of a holiday seals off
another year. Younger, we hesitated
over decisions that closed doors. Now doors
slam behind us of their own accord.
Driving home at night we see on the outskirts
the darkness lit by fires where the town's waste is burnt.
We drive on to the security of street lights,
a familiar haven that has come
to take on significance.

NIGHT OMENS

Impinging on the cocoon of sleep:
The heavy breathing of the sea;
The interminable chirping of crickets;
The drunken return of revellers;
A great dog gnawing on bones
in a deserted side street.

WRIST

A sudden stumble down a steep path
the wrist taking the full weight,
sinews wrenched,
and several of those small bones
given a quick shuffle.
For a week or so it shrieked
like a toothache at the end of an arm.

That was a while ago,
and now, after resting and some care,
it's back in service again.
But catch it off guard,
or strain it at the wrong angle,
and it will let you know all right.

Until then
we'd got on pretty well,
this body and I.
Up here, I made the decisions,
gave the orders,
it served its turn.

And in return I cared for it,
fed it and gave it a break
every so often.
It had its limitations of course:
No four minute miles,
lifting ton weights
or stuff like that,
and throw down too much alcohol
and it would play up a bit.

Yet on the whole, I'd say
it had been a satisfactory relationship.
It did its job,
and let me get on with the important ones.

But now, something
at the far end of one arm
has made a difference.
An unthinking twist
or an awkward pressure
and it sends back a sharp
unignorable protest of pain,
upsetting the flow
of a planned operation,
or intruding upon
an objective appraisal.

It's getting that one can't
afford to ignore it.

Things may, of course,
get back to normal in time:
but meanwhile
I'll have to adjust to it.

SNOW

Night's end, we emerged
To a world transformed.
Snow's wafers,
As unsummoned
And as transcending as love,
Silently fallen.
A blanket simplicity,
The purities lay before us.
But already
The footprints are ours.

MY TRISTAN AND I

Oh my loved leaper!
my stream seducer!
Mark would have sliced you
to the marrow and left you bereft
if he'd ever caught you.
For it was more than a footprint you left,
or the snaring flour
you sifted
in your vaulting hour,
and more than the stream that lifted
my skirts when we tumbled
at Mal Plas.
What quick passionate eel
could I feel
warming those icy waters?
Such an acrobatic and ingenious love,
its edge honed by danger,
was all a Queen could ask
from a nephew and no stranger.
Though there were times
I wished it could be
a little less athletic
and a shade more leisurely.

ENCOUNTERING THE MUSE

There is a time for returning to forests
that retain a darkness
profounder than disenchantment,
engendering depths where the hold
on reality slips and concepts crumble
like the treasure in a suddenly unsealed tomb.
The memory traverses the stations of pain
to where lakes steam in the cold air
and somewhere the she-poet lurks
in shades neglected by the mind,
the salt of her flesh arousing all senses.

THE VOYAGE OF THE BEAGLE

'Why, the shape of his head is quite altered'
   Dr. Darwin on his son's return to England.

And where was that other germ contracted?
From the great bones in the gravel at Punta Alba
Or the buckled blackness of the Galapagos?
Deeper than the Benchuga, truth bites
Consuming as a cancer, shapes changing
With the shifting continents of faith.
If the Greek was right: who pursues what?
Certainly, there was no sudden revelation:
But a prolonged teetering on the edge of discovery
Where ideas reverberate as did sounds
In the clear air of the Andes.
The *Beagle* and Fitzroy departed,
Here at Down House the voyage continues
To the same end, a voyage without end.

UNCLE TOM

"I'll tell you what we'll do boy,
Get two ponies, camping gear and food,
And, travelling light, each night we'll camp
Where day's end finds us.
You'll like that, the camp fires and the woods."
And there's no doubt I would have done.

Often we talked of it,
My uncle and I. He fresh-faced,
With something of the countryman,
Though if he had ever been such
I'm not sure. He could certainly ride well,
Sit a horse, I'll say that.
Learnt as a trooper in the cavalry.

Often I dreamed of it:
Lush lazy days beside a pony,
Sleeping under stars, and the bright mornings
Wonderfully fresh, the freedom and the air;
But they never came.
And, as in time, I knew they never would,
I didn't hold it against him,

Those promises, the hopes he raised.
Even now, the boy near two score on,
Uncle long dead, I occasionally remember
And gain some pleasure from it.

BEAST

Why did the grey climacteric beast choose this time
To make iron forest of the country of the soul?
Lumbering into our lives, its great foot-prints
In the ooze of our susceptibilities,
It pushes and crushes, this ton of pachydermic pig,
Leaning with a sigh of laboured air
Hot with the stench of fermenting jungles.
Insensitive as stones the small eyes stare
From the mud-caked plates of its armoured hide,
As it blunders out of a primaeval past
Into the thunder of its blustering charge.
And at just the wrong time. Or is it always so?
Though they say the horn it bears still retains
Regenerative magic. Have we come to this
That only our superstitions can help us?

HORSES AT DAWN

With the patience of trees
That is beyond endurance,
They stand the night out
Cocooned in the redolence
Of their condensing breath,
To appear at day-break
Like dark islands
In the long lines of mist
That form on the meadows.
Stoicism, even fatalism
Are concepts
They have no truck with,
Who measure time in dawns
And beneficence in a rise
Of small degrees.

EXPLORERS

Evening, and warm from discarded clothing
she approaches, her acid mingling
with the fading unguents of the morning's toilet.
Above an affrontary of legs, her waist still fret
with the indentations of elastic,
her outstretched arms offer the ministrations
of those comfortably hirsute shadows.
Stirring towards explorations
of sinuosities
we discover something of the other's reality:
and, if aware,
catch a glimpse of our own.

TERRAIN

(For Rigby Graham)

Isolating the walled cities
Lie the great plains
Unprotected from winds
That hone their knives
On the ancient bones
Of the earth.
The deserts where fear
And the lack of pasture
Keep men moving: and
The need for companionship is ultimate.
With their sparse grasses
Of the consistency of wire,
And the rare arthritic tree,
They offer passage only
To marauding hoards,
And speak of afflictions
That move closer.

NIGHT TRAIN

Night train and the passing lights
Of windows, roads and factories
Where WRIGLEYS
In large red block neon
Ignites a darkness
Beyond which lurk
The real creatures of the night.
Continuing, the parallel of rails
Meets only in the mind.
We touch hands, realizing
How we seem to spend all our time
In saying goodbye.

OLD

A man's history locked in his head:
A war, a marriage, a father long dead,
And Sunday dinner with the family.
Now it's one place set, two bangers
And a boiled spud the lone economy
In a room where the clock ticks noisily;
The bits of furniture for friends, and letters
Less than occasionally from a daughter
Whose face is fading in America.
How long can it last
The cracked cistern of the memory?
Too slow, and yet too full of the past
To let a future in.

IN TIME OF 'THE BREAKING OF NATIONS'

'a damned nice thing':   Wellington

In the Russian campaign of 1812,
Because of a retention of urine,
Napoleon held up his advance for several days,
And on the eve of Waterloo
He was suddenly incapacitated by piles,
While his irascibility,
Aggravated by constipation,
Was reflected in outbursts of temper
On members of his staff.
On such did the fate of nations hang:
Or is that what was called
God being on our side?

LADDERMEN (a cultural exchange)

On a razor clear Mediterranean morning,
While I was on my way to queue at the baker's,
A Spanish workman, high on a ladder,
Cementing breeze-blocks to make apartments,
Filled the air with his whistling
Of 'Winchester Cathedral'.

While in the stone embraced clarity of that edifice,
On the other side from where one walks
On the memorial to Jane Austen,
Is an inscription to the leader
Of the ladder party at Sevastopol.
What he whistled is not recorded.

RAJ

Long before the lowering of flags
it was already dying.
In the mess the fading sepia
of polo teams, a subscription
still obligatory
though there were no ponies.

The pipe band on Sundays
and Mozart on records
in the officers' club.

Not far and a stiff climb
the caves where in their darkness
the many armed Shiva
still dances, *Tandava*,
his power surviving
in the universal lingam,

and a Greek inscription
reminds that others had been before
                  and departed.
As Akbar's Gate of Victory
                  still stands

(he never returning)

> *The world is a bridge*
> *pass over it*
> *but build no house here.*

Elsewhere the town plans of the Indus Valley.

In the city the white caps of Congress
punctuated the crowds
on betel mottled pavements
near somebody else's
Gateway to India,
while sculptured millenial lovers

continued to fondle
their moon-breasted paramours,
and holy bathers
courted cholera and immortality
in that order.

What now remains?
The uniforms, the language
of Shakespeare Wallah
alongside the Vedas,
mother of Sanskrit and
grandmother of languages,

who produced it here?

the ciphered Victorian pillar-boxes at Ooty
and the English country graveyards.

Yet Shiva too is a haunter of cemeteries.
The past haunting us
as it always haunts the present.

here is another bond to break

But India, as Gandhi insisted,
is to be found in the villages:
in the cool first air of morning,
the jasmine and joss of the bazaar
above which bats hang from the trees
like great leathern fruit,
the cave-ribbed oxen,
the dry-dust roads
and the tenacity to survive
a poverty the West has forgotten.

And carved long before
into the rock of the hillside
Ganeśa,
      the elephant-headed pathfinder
      and protector of crossroads,
stands guard
      as with evening
intruders depart
with the heat of the day
to leave that which endures
to reassert itself.

The Photograph Poems: The photograph of Keith Douglas is to be found in *Poetry London X*; and that of Gertrude and Alice is on the back of a dust wrapper of a book of Alice's.

My Tristan and I: The incidents referred to are to be found in the French poet Béroul's early and more robust version of the legends.

Raj: Tandava is Shiva's dance in which he represents the destruction of the illusory world of Maya, the illusion of material reality.

Lines 22-24 are taken from the inscription on Akbar's Gate of Victory, Fatephur Sikri.

Line 43 is from the Upanishads.

Line 49 is a supposed saying of the Buddha.